party bites

Lydia France
photography by Jean Cazals

party bites
 easy recipes for fingerfood & party snacks

RYLAND
PETERS
& SMALL
LONDON NEW YORK

Dedication
To my mother and father for their
love and guidance.

Senior Designer Carl Hodson
Commissioning Editor Julia Charles
Production Controller Hazel Kirkman
Art Director Leslie Harrington
Publishing Director Alison Starling

Food Stylists Maxine Clark, Linda Tubby,
& Katie Rogers
Prop Stylists Sue Rowlands & Rachel Jukes
Index Sandra Shotter

Author's acknowledgments
Thank you to the team at Ryland Peters
& Small—Julia Charles, Carl Hodson, and
Alison Starling—plus Maxine Clark for
gorgeous food styling and Jean Cazals for
the beautiful photography. Thanks also go
to my husband and parents for being guinea
pigs, and to Jean and Mary, for their years of
support and honest feedback.

First published in the
United States in 2008
by Ryland Peters & Small Inc.
519 Broadway, 5th Floor
New York, NY 10012
www.rylandpeters.com

Text © Lydia France 2008
Design and photographs
© Ryland Peters & Small 2008

All photography by Jean Cazals except:
page 4 David Loftus, page 6 Noel Murphy,
page 9 Peter Cassidy. Image used on pages
2–3, 4–5, 12–13, 26–27, 46–47, 66–67, 82–83
© Jenny Kennedy-Olsen

10 9 8 7 6 5 4 3 2 1

Printed in China

Notes
• All spoon measurements are
level unless otherwise specified.
• Ovens should be preheated to
the specified temperatures. All
ovens work slightly differently.
We recommend using an oven
thermometer and suggest you
consult the manufacturer's
handbook for any special
instructions, particularly if you
are cooking in a fan-assisted
oven, as you will probably need to
adjust temperatures according to
the manufacturer's instructions.

Library of Congress Cataloging-in-
Publication Data

France, Lydia.
  Party bites : easy recipes for
fingerfood and party snacks / Lydia
France ; photography by Jean Cazals.
    p. cm.
Includes index.
ISBN 978-1-84597-710-8
  1. Appetizers. 2. Entertaining.
3. Snack foods. I. Title.
TX740.F658 2008
641.8'12—dc22
                              2008021720

secrets of a successful party

The finest food I have ever eaten at a party was fresh, vibrant, and perfectly seasoned. As with any sort of cooking, good party food comes down to the quality of the ingredients, imagination of the cook, and skilful execution.

The canapé has invariably mirrored the mood of the time and has, like fashion, changed its countenance many times throughout the decades. I was delighted to be asked to write this book as, through my work as a caterer, I have witnessed many of these changing trends over the last 20 years. Increasingly today other countries and cultures are lending their culinary secrets to us which has widened our scope for experimentation further and given us a treasure trove of new flavors to work with.

For impact and big taste, I like to choose foods which are in season and flavors which marry together well. When planning a new party menu, I visit a food market for inspiration. I feel the food I'm buying for firmness and ripeness, smell it and wherever possible, taste it. A good piece of advice I overheard while waiting in line at a cheese shop was; "You cook at your best if you cook the food you like eating yourself" so don't be afraid of serving tried and tested favorites. That said, it's good to try something new, but do practice first until you get it right. The recipes in this book are all designed to be simple to follow but it still pays to have a dummy run when you're catering for large numbers of people so that you be confident on the day.

Presentation also plays a huge part in hosting a memorable party. The food ought to be eye-catching, dramatic, and appetizing. Give yourself time to consider how you want to present your food. Look for inspiration in magazines and books, experiment with ideas, and invest in some stylish new serving plates or dishes. Choose colors that will compliment each other and be artistic with the food itself—whether you arrange it simply or elaborately on the plate, in neat and tidy rows, bold tumbling towers, or statement-making stacks. Decorations and garnishes such as herbs, flowers, fruit, leaves, or chiles should always be in keeping with the occasion as well as clean and non-toxic.

I hope this book offers you plenty of achievable yet impressive ideas and will perhaps inspire you to try out some new recipes next time you entertain. You too can enjoy the experience of seeing your guests' eyes light up, their eager fingers seizing the tasting morsels on display, and then offering their heartfelt gratitude to you for hosting a wonderful and enjoyable party. Here are a few basic guidelines and some useful advice, to help you when planning a party:

Match the occasion and the food to the time of year. Seasonal food is much more inviting—light, fresh food in the warmth of summer and comforting food when it's miserable and cold. Always have a Plan B if it's an outdoor event—you can never guarantee the weather.

For large numbers of guests and very special occasions it is worth thinking about hiring a few waiting staff to take coats, serve food and drink, help with the clearing up, and generally ensure the smooth running of your party. If your budget doesn't run to professional staff,

don't be afraid to ask a few good friends to help. If there's a task to be done on the day, such as taking coats or pouring drinks, delegate and get them involved. The last thing you want to do is to spend all of your time running around or locked away in the kitchen. Find time to relax and enjoy the party, there's no point in entertaining if you don't!

Check your equipment—it's rare to have enough glasses, serving platters, napkins, or toothpicks to cater for a crowd so make sure that you buy, hire, or borrow enough for your purposes. Some wine shops now offer a glass hire service—play it safe and allow two wine glasses per head in case of mishaps or switches from white to red wine, etc. You may also need ice and large buckets or bins to keep wine or sodas cool. If you find you need a large quantity of ice, it's more practical to buy it than to try and make it in your own freezer.

Calculate how much food you will need —for a typical drinks party, you'll want to provide an average of eight different choices and allow about two of each per person. Try to balance your selection by offering something for everyone, for example: two fish, two meat, one cheese, one vegetable, and a sweet one (see pages 10–11 for a helpful Menu Planner). Don't forget to check if any of your guests have any food allergies or specific dietary requirements. Always let guests know if food contains nuts and offer a vegan

option if necessary. If you have young children coming, it's a good idea to have some very simple foods to offer, such as bowls of cherry tomatoes or chips and breadsticks with dips.

Get organized ahead of time—draw up a detailed shopping list and make sure that you can know where to source any more unusual ingredients. You may even need to order some of these online if they are not stocked locally, so think ahead

and allow sufficient time for delivery. If you need a particular cut of meat or type of fish, order it in advance from your butcher or fishmonger and make arrangements to collect it close to the day of your party.

Get ahead on the food preparation— wherever possible make a few of your chosen canapés (or elements of, such as tartlet shells) in advance and refrigerate or freeze them until needed.

Food hygiene and safety—this is crucial when you are catering for a party. Bear in mind these important health and safety guidelines: check use-by dates, keep all surfaces, counters and equipment spotlessly clean, always store cooked foods and raw foods separately, keep food covered and protected until needed, and wash your hands frequently.

Do not be tempted to place a glass, or anything else, on a serving plate with he food to collect used sticks, olive pits, bones, or any other food debris—it looks messy and uninviting. Instead, pass

around a separate dish to collect any rubbish or place small bowls or cups on tables around the room, along with piles of clean napkins.

Choosing drinks—good choices for a drinks party are Champagne or sparkling wine or a light, refreshing white and a soft, fruity red. Avoid wines that are heavily oaked or high in alcohol, which can easily result in your guests drinking more than they realize. If you're holding an outdoor event in summer, rosé wine or a pink sparkling wine is a popular choice. Allow about 1–1½ hours in the fridge to chill white wine and 1½–2 hours for Champagne or other sparkling wines. A reasonable amount to cater for is half a bottle per head, although if a party is due to go on for quite a time or you have guests who are likely to drink rather more than that, allow a bottle each in total. Always offer two to three different non-alcoholic drinks, such as a fresh juice, soda, and a flavored seltzer, along with plenty of pitchers of ice water.

menu planner

Here are a few suggested fingerfood and party bite menus for a selection of typical parties and gatherings. Each has a good balance of flavors, textures, colors, and choices. The foods have been chosen to suit the tastes of the guests you'd expect to find at each occasion described.

Note that V denotes a vegetarian option.

Champagne Reception

This menu features quintessentially "modern vintage" canapés perfect for any elegant occasion, such as an engagement or wedding anniversary party.

Oak-smoked salmon with ginger butter on oat crackers (page 80)
Smoked haddock and celeriac on pumpernickel with beet relish (page 68)
Arugula sandwiches (page 79)
Lemon buffalo mozzarella and pickled figs on crostini (page 21)
Coconut and cardamom chicken (page 52)
Hot crumbed shrimp with tomato aioli (page 55)
Beef tenderloin on toast with mustard and arugula (page 18)
Mini meringues brushed with bitter chocolate (page 88)

Chic Cocktail Party

Here is a selection of sophisticated eats guaranteed to add style and glamour to any party.

Vermouth scallops with green olive tapenade (page 43)
Anchovy wafers (see page 71)
Harissa hummus with pomegranate vinaigrette (page 36)
Parsnip and sage phyllo wraps (page 39)
Spanish men (page 64)
Sticky dates with lemon feta and walnuts (page 40)
Peppered duck, fig, and bay skewers (page 59)
Mini meringues brushed with bitter chocolate (page 88)

The Coordinated Party for Busy Hosts

This menu can be prepared with minimum fuss but still guarantees maximum impact. All of the food can be prepped in advance, is easily assembled or simple to cook.

Shrimp cocktail shots (page 60)
Manchego marinated with thyme and juniper (page 64)
Anchovy wafers (page 71)
Harissa hummus with pomegranate vinaigrette (page 36)
Coconut and cardamom chicken (page 52)
Sticky dates with lemon feta and chorizo (page 40)
Chicken salad kabobs (page 63)
Snowy pine nut cookies (page 91)

Summer Drinks in the Garden
These tasty bites are all refreshing, piquant, and aromatic,
making them the perfect choice for summer "al fresco" parties.

Arugula sandwiches (page 79)
Manchego marinated with thyme and juniper (page 79)
Twice-marinated salt lime chicken (page 63)
Parmesan and sweet paprika crackers (page 72)
Broiled lamb skewers with garlic and saffron custard
  (page 51)
Piri piri mushrooms (page 56)
Hot crumbed shrimp with tomato aioli (page 55)
Rose marzipan dates (page 84)
Peppered pineapple, coconut, and rum shots (page 95)

Girls' Night In
The perfect solution for any girls-only gathering, whether it's a bridal
or baby shower or just an excuse to get together and enjoy a chat with
a glass of wine and some tasty snacks.

Oak-smoked salmon with ginger butter on oat biscuits
  (page 80)
Harissa hummus with pomegranate vinaigrette (page 36)
Caesar salad tarts (page 14)
Chicken salad kabobs (page 63)
Spiced pork balls with sticky cider syrup (page 48)
Slow-roasted tomato galettes with black olive tapenade
  and goat cheese (page 25)
Fudgy nuts (page 84)

Informal Drinks with Friends and Family
Ideal food for a relaxed party—satisfy your hungry family
and friends with these generously proportioned bites.

Black bean chili in polenta cups with sour cream
  (page 17)
Harissa hummus with pomegranate vinaigrette (page 36)
Trio of honey-baked Camembert with Calvados and herbs
  (page 28)
Cheese scones with cheddar and pickled pears (page 76)
Flash-seared tuna on rye with horseradish and tarragon
  cream (page 75)
Sesame maple turkey fingers (page 35)
Orange and chocolate marble cake (page 87)

Christmas Drinks Party
This festive, colorful, and indulgent menu will tempt and treat
your guests during the holiday season.

Butternut squash hot shots (page 44)
Smoked haddock and celeriac on pumpernickel
  with beet relish (page 68)
Parsnip and sage phyllo wraps (page 39)
Shrimp cocktail shots (page 60)
Sesame maple turkey fingers (page 35)
Piquant rare duck in endive boats with crushed
  peanuts (page 31)
Apple and Calvados pies (page 92)
Fudgy nuts (page 84)

tartlets & toasts

caesar salad tarts

Makes 40–50

13 slices fresh white bread

3 tablespoons olive oil, shaken with 1 crushed garlic clove and 1 teaspoon sea salt

3½ oz. anchovy fillets, chopped quite finely

1 garlic clove, crushed

1 tablespoon snipped fresh dill

1 tablespoon chopped fresh mint

1 small head Boston lettuce, finely shredded

grated peel and freshly squeezed juice of 1 unwaxed lime

1–2 egg yolks (optional)

1 cup finely grated Parmesan cheese

freshly ground black pepper

a 2-inch cookie cutter

4 or 5 x 12-hole mini muffin pans

For those who like the garlicky crouton bit of Caesar Salad best. Here the crouton is the star, with the salad cradled within. Use Boston lettuce, as it holds its bite and freshness well, even when chopped.

Preheat the oven to 400°F.

Use a 2-inch cookie cutter to cut 3 or 4 rounds out of each slice of bread. Brush each round with the garlic oil and press into mini muffin pans. Bake for about 6 minutes until golden brown and toasted.

Put any remaining garlic oil in a large bowl with all the other ingredients, except the Parmesan, and toss together.

Finally, sprinkle the Parmesan into the salad to coat everything finely and pile into the crouton cases.

black bean chili in polenta cups with sour cream

Makes about 60

POLENTA CUPS

1 stick plus 4 tablespoons butter

¾ cup cream cheese

2 cups plus 2 tablespoons all-purpose flour

1 cup plus 2 tablespoons polenta

a pinch of sea salt crystals

BLACK BEAN CHILI

1 lb. dried black beans, soaked in water overnight

2 teaspoons cumin seeds

2 teaspoons coriander seeds

2–3 tablespoons olive oil

4 shallots, finely chopped

3 garlic cloves, crushed

1 fresh green chile, chopped

1 fresh red chile, chopped

1 teaspoon soft brown sugar

2 teaspoons sea salt

2 oz. bittersweet chocolate, grated

1 tablespoon tomato concentrate

1 tablespoon chopped cilantro

1⅔ cups sour cream

Spanish smoked paprika, to serve

4 or 5 x 12-hole mini muffin pans

This canapé is so useful because the cups and chili can be made in advance. The polenta cups can be frozen, while the black bean chili can be made on the day and kept in the fridge for a couple of hours, then warmed through when you are ready to assemble and serve it.

Preheat the oven to 350°F.

First make the polenta cups. Cream the butter and cream cheese together. Combine the flour, polenta, and salt and add to the butter and cream cheese gradually, until the mixture forms a dough. Break off 1½ inch balls and neatly press into the mini muffin pans, forming a cup shape. Bake for 20 minutes until golden.

To make the chili, put the drained black beans in a large saucepan of fresh cold water, bring to a boil, and cook for 1–1½ hours until tender. In a large heavy-based saucepan warm the spice seeds until just starting to pop, then remove from the pan and set aside. Gently heat the olive oil in the same pan and add the shallots, garlic, and chiles. After 5 minutes add the sugar, salt, chocolate, and tomato concentrate and cook for a further couple of minutes.

Remove from the heat and let cool slightly, then blend in a food processor with the warmed spice seeds. Combine this mixture, the drained black beans, and cilantro in a large bowl. Spoon into the polenta cups, top with sour cream, and sprinkle over a little paprika.

beef tenderloin on toast with mustard and arugula

1 ciabatta loaf

2 tablespoons whole-grain mustard

2 tablespoons homemade mayonnaise or prepared mayonnaise

14 oz. beef tenderloin

1 tablespoon olive oil

2 handfuls of arugula

sea salt and cracked black pepper, to serve

a stovetop grill pan

A satisfying combination of rare, juicy beef with mustard and peppery arugula. If you prefer, Dijon, English, or honey mustard can be substituted for whole-grain mustard.

Preheat the oven to 400°F.

Cut the ciabatta loaf in half lengthwise and toast in the oven for about 10 minutes. Mix the mustard and mayonnaise together and spread evenly onto the cut halves of toasted ciabatta.

Brush the beef with the olive oil and heat a stovetop grill pan. Sear the beef in the hot pan without disturbing, for about 2 minutes, and repeat on the other side. Transfer the beef to a chopping board and let rest for 15 minutes.

Using a sharp knife, slice the beef into enough thin slices to cover the ciabatta. Press the beef gently onto the ciabatta, to encourage it to stick to the mustard mixture. Scatter the arugula over the beef and carefully cut into fingers. Serve with little dishes of sea salt and cracked black pepper.

lemon buffalo mozzarella and pickled figs on crostini

Makes about 20

PICKLED FIGS

1⅔ cups rosé wine

6 tablespoons sweet raspberry vinegar

1 small fresh red chile

1 clove

6 dried lavender heads

10 soft dried figs, quartered

LEMON BUFFALO MOZZARELLA

2–3 tablespoons extra virgin olive oil

grated peel and freshly squeezed juice of 1 small unwaxed lemon

1 teaspoon sea salt crystals

8 oz. buffalo mozzarella (about 2 balls)

CROSTINI

1–2 baguettes, each cut into ½ inch slices

baking sheets

When you can get them, ripe figs are a delicious alternative to dried. Only use the best, freshest buffalo mozzarella for this recipe. This topping also works well on toasted ciabatta.

To make the pickled figs, put all the ingredients except the figs in a saucepan and reduce the liquid by half over medium heat. Remove from the heat, add the figs, and let cool.

For the mozzarella, pour the olive oil into a bowl and mix with the lemon peel and juice, and the salt crystals. Tear the mozzarella in half and in half again, repeating until you have enough pieces to match your fig halves. If the mozzarella is very soft, tear it in half then cut it with scissors. Gently coat the mozzarella in the lemon mixture and leave for 1 hour to infuse.

Preheat the oven to 400°F. To make the crostini, bake the bread slices on baking sheets in the oven for about 10–15 minutes until golden.

To assemble, put a piece of infused mozzarella and a pickled fig quarter on each crostini so they lean against each other. Serve immediately.

crab and ricotta toasts with chive, caper, and radish salsa

Makes 40

1 baguette

1 lb. fresh lump crabmeat

6½ oz. fresh ricotta or farmer cheese

CHIVE, CAPER, AND RADISH SALSA

6 oz. tiny radishes, roughly chopped

½ cup capers, drained and chopped

½ cup snipped fresh chives

4 tablespoons olive oil

4 tablespoons green ginger wine (such as Stone's) or sweet sherry plus ¼ teaspoon ground ginger

baking sheets

Present a few of these toasts with the salsa on top as they look so pretty. Fresh crab is delicious in its own right, so serve the rest of the salsa in a bowl with a small serving spoon so your guests can add as much or little as they wish.

Preheat the oven to 400°F.

Slice the baguette into 40 even slices and bake on baking sheets in the oven for about 10 minutes, until browned.

Gently combine the fresh crabmeat and ricotta in a bowl and chill. When you are ready to serve, mix all the salsa ingredients together in a separate bowl. Use a small palette knife to spread the cold crab mixture onto the toasts, then top with a little salsa. Serve immediately.

slow-roasted tomato galettes with black olive tapenade and goat cheese

Makes 40–50

20–25 baby plum tomatoes

1 tablespoon superfine sugar

14 oz. puff pastry dough, thawed if frozen

¼ cup olive oil

5-oz. goat cheese log with rind (not too ripe)

freshly ground black pepper

small fresh basil leaves, to serve

BLACK OLIVE TAPENADE

⅔ cup pitted black olives

2 tablespoons capers

1 tablespoon anchovy paste

1 garlic clove, crushed

1 tablespoon olive oil

1 teaspoon sea salt

1 teaspoon chopped fresh thyme

oiled baking sheets

a 1½-inch cookie cutter

I would recommend making more of these sweet-tasting tomatoes than you need! Replace the tomatoes and tapenade with slow-roasted black grapes and onion confit as an alternative idea.

Preheat the oven to 275°F.

Cut the baby plum tomatoes in half lengthwise, season with the sugar and black pepper, and put on an oiled baking sheet. Bake in the oven for 2 hours. Remove the tomatoes from the oven and leave to cool.

Turn the oven temperature up to 400°F. Brush the puff pastry dough with the olive oil, prick all over with a fork, and stamp out 40–50 discs using a 1½ inch cookie cutter, and put them on baking sheets. Cook for 10–15 minutes, turning over halfway through. Remove from the oven but leave the heat on.

Put all the tapenade ingredients in a food processor and blend to mix. Cover and set aside until needed.

Thinly slice the goat cheese into 40–50 rounds or pieces depending on the diameter of the log (to make this easier, chill the cheese beforehand).

To assemble the galettes, spread a little tapenade onto each cooked pastry disc. Top with a goat cheese slice and tomato half. Return to the oven for about 5 minutes to warm through, then serve topped with a basil leaf.

dips & fingers

trio of honey-baked camembert with calvados and herbs

Serves about 15

3 x 8 oz. Camembert cheeses
in boxes
3 tablespoons Calvados or brandy
3 tablespoons dark honey
1 fat garlic clove, sliced
3 fresh sage leaves
3 sprigs fresh rosemary
3 fresh bay leaves

TO SERVE
celery ribs
walnut bread
chilled tiny radishes

This molten cheese dish is spiked with perfumed honey, pungent Calvados, and garlic. Serve with crunchy celery ribs, warm crusty walnut bread, and chilled radishes.

Preheat the oven to 400°F.

Unwrap the cheeses and return them to their boxes. Using a skewer, make 6 or 7 holes in each cheese. Mix the Calvados and honey together and spoon the mixture into and over the holes. Stud with the garlic slices and lightly press the sage, rosemary, and bay onto each cheese. Bake for about 7 minutes.

Remove the boxes from the oven. Using sharp scissors, quickly make 3 cuts on the surface of each cheese, from the center out, and gently open the "petals" a little. Take the cheeses out of their boxes, put them on a plate and serve straight away.

piquant rare duck in endive boats with crushed peanuts

Makes about 30

14 oz. boneless duck breast, skin on

2 tablespoons red currant jelly

1 teaspoon finely chopped fresh red chile

2 teaspoons smoked Spanish paprika

2 garlic cloves, crushed

2 teaspoons sweet raspberry vinegar

3–4 medium Belgian endives

a handful of fresh basil leaves

⅔ cup dry-roasted peanuts, roughly crushed in a food processor

Look for small to medium heads of Belgian endive to make good-sized "boats" for this recipe. As an alternative finishing touch, try scattering over a mix of crushed salted peanuts and freshly grated coconut.

Preheat the oven to 400°F.

Score the duck fat (not the flesh) with a sharp knife. Cook in a hot flameproof, ovenproof pan over medium/high heat until the skin is golden brown and most of the fat has been rendered. Transfer to the oven for 10 minutes, then remove and leave to rest.

Meanwhile, mix the red currant jelly, chile, paprika, garlic, and vinegar together in a bowl. Remove and discard any remaining cold fat from the duck breasts, then cut them into equal slices. Put the duck slices in the bowl containing the chile mixture and toss to coat the duck.

Cut the thick ends off the endive and separate the leaves. Line each one with a basil leaf, put a rare slice of duck on top, and scatter the peanuts over. Serve with the pointed end of the leaf facing outwards on the plate.

warm spice-rubbed potatoes with rosemary mayonnaise

Serves 50

ROSEMARY MAYONNAISE

3 egg yolks

3 tablespoons fresh rosemary needles

1 teaspoon Dijon mustard

3 tablespoons cider vinegar

2 cups grapeseed oil

SPICE-RUBBED POTATOES

1½ lbs. pink-skinned new potatoes, halved lengthwise

1 teaspoon cayenne pepper

1 teaspoon caraway seeds

1 teaspoon coriander seeds

a small piece of cinnamon stick

1 garlic clove, crushed

1 teaspoon sea salt

2 tablespoons olive oil

a baking sheet

This recipe uses pink-skinned new potatoes for their charming color and firm texture. If they're not available, you can substitute any large potatoes, peeled, and cut to your preferred size.

To make the mayonnaise, put all the ingredients, except the grapeseed oil, in a food processor and blend. With the motor running, slowly add the oil in droplets until the mayonnaise starts to thicken. Continue with an even trickle until you have incorporated all the oil. Spoon into a bowl and chill.

For the potatoes, cook the potatoes in a large pan of boiling water for about 12–15 minutes, until almost cooked. Drain and pat dry. Gently warm the spices in a small pan for about 2 minutes until their scent starts to pervade the kitchen. Put the warmed spices, garlic, and salt in the clean food processor and blend to make a rough spice mix.

Preheat the oven to 400°F. Put the potatoes in a bowl with the olive oil and toss together. Using clean hands, rub the spice mixture onto the potatoes and bake them on a baking sheet in the preheated oven for about 20 minutes until golden. Serve with a generous dollop of rosemary mayonnaise.

sesame maple turkey fingers

Makes about 40

4 tablespoons maple syrup, plus
3 tablespoons extra for dipping

1 small fresh red chile, halved,
seeded, and finely chopped

1 teaspoon sea salt

1 garlic clove, crushed

1 lb. lean turkey breast meat

1 cup sesame seeds,
lightly toasted

fresh mint leaves, to scatter

baking sheets

The maple syrup will only subtly flavor the turkey, so offer more in a bowl as a dipping sauce. If you're entertaining children, omit the chile and garlic from the recipe and they will love the turkey fingers.

Put the maple syrup, half the chile, the salt, and garlic in a bowl and leave for 30 minutes.

Preheat the oven to 400°F.

Cut the turkey breast into strips (about 40 in total). Coat the turkey fingers with the maple syrup mixture, then with the sesame seeds. Arrange the fingers slightly apart on baking sheets and cook for about 8 minutes, until cooked through.

Put the remaining chile and 3 tablespoons maple syrup in a small bowl as a dipping sauce. Scatter the mint leaves over the turkey and serve.

harissa hummus with pomegranate vinaigrette

Serves 20–30

1 lb. (3 cups) dried chickpeas, soaked in water overnight

½ cup tahini

2 teaspoons harissa (Moroccan hot chile paste)

6 garlic cloves

grated peel of 2 unwaxed lemons and freshly squeezed juice of 4

sea salt

POMEGRANATE VINAIGRETTE

seeds from 1 pomegranate

2 tablespoons dark honey

2 big handfuls flat-leaf parsley, chopped

8–10 tablespoons extra virgin olive oil

sea salt, to taste

3 tablespoons toasted sesame seeds, to serve

Homemade hummus is quite a different beast from its store-bought equivalent—much bigger on both flavor and texture. This version is big on looks too. Serve at room temperature with toasts and flatbreads.

Put the drained chickpeas in a pan of fresh, unsalted, cold water. Bring to a boil and cook for 1½ hours until soft. Drain, reserving the cooking water, and reserve ½ cup of the chickpeas to serve.

In a food processor, blend the remaining chickpeas and all the other ingredients, except the salt, to a soft purée, adding a little of the cooking water at a time until you have a smooth paste. Taste and season with salt. Transfer to a large shallow bowl.

Gently combine all the pomegranate vinaigrette ingredients in a bowl and add the reserved chickpeas. Spoon this mixture onto the hummus. Scatter the toasted sesame seeds over the top to serve.

parsnip and sage phyllo wraps

Makes 32

4 parsnips, peeled

8 sheets filo pastry dough, plus a few extra in case of tearing

1 stick plus 4 tablespoons butter, melted

32 large fresh sage leaves

sea salt and freshly ground black pepper

baking sheets

Here the starchy sweetness of parsnips marries beautifully with musky sage and crisp, buttery phyllo pastry. Don't worry if yours do not look quite as neat as the ones shown here—they will still taste delicious! These wraps also look good served standing in a small glass pitcher.

Cut the peeled parsnips lengthwise into quarters, remove the hard central core, and cut each quarter lengthwise again, leaving you with 32 lengths of parsnip. Blanch these for 1 minute in a saucepan of boiling water, drain and let cool.

Preheat the oven to 400°F. Brush a sheet of phyllo pastry with melted butter and grind a little salt and pepper evenly over the top. Cut into quarters and put a large sage leaf (or 2 small sage leaves) on each piece. Put a parsnip strip at one edge of the pastry and roll up to form a long thin cigar, tucking the ends in as neatly as possible. Repeat this with the remaining sheets of phyllo dough.

Lay the phyllo wraps on baking sheets and brush with the remaining butter. Bake for about 20 minutes or until golden and crisp.

sticky dates with lemon feta and walnuts

Makes 40

7 oz. Greek feta cheese

grated peel of 1 unwaxed lemon and freshly squeezed juice of ½

20 Medjool dates, halved and pitted

⅔ cup walnut halves or diced chorizo sausage

sea salt and freshly ground black pepper

fresh mint leaves, to serve

These canapés are refreshing, zesty, and perfect with cocktails. Put the finished dates in the freezer for 5 minutes before serving; it somehow intensifies their honeyed sweetness. For meat lovers or those with nut allergies, chorizo is a great substitute for the walnuts.

Cut the feta into 40 little blocks or mash it, as preferred. Put in a bowl with the grated lemon peel and juice and add salt to taste. Let stand for 30 minutes, turning occasionally.

Put a block or a small amount of mashed feta at one end of each date half, then add a walnut half to overlap the cheese. Grind a little black pepper over the top and finish with a mint leaf.

vermouth scallops with green olive tapenade

Makes 30–40

1 lb. fresh scallops (30–40)

3 tablespoons dry vermouth

2 tablespoons olive oil

⅔ cup pitted green olives

3 scallions, chopped

1 garlic clove

1 tablespoon chopped fresh flat-leaf parsley

1 cured chorizo sausage (about 10 oz.)

sea salt and freshly ground black pepper

a stovetop grill pan

toothpicks

Confirmed martini lovers will enjoy this one; it's a fitting canapé to kick off a party. These can also be served on slices of cucumber; one large cucumber is sufficient for this quantity of scallops.

Put the scallops in a large bowl with 1 tablespoon of the vermouth, the olive oil, and a pinch of salt and black pepper and let sit for 10 minutes.

Heat a stovetop grill pan over high heat until very hot and sear the scallops for 1 minute on each side. Do not move the scallops during cooking, or they will tear.

Put all the remaining ingredients, except the chorizo, in a food processor with ½ teaspoon salt and give it a few short sharp blasts until the tapenade mixture looks chopped but not too mushy. Slice the chorizo so you have a slice for each scallop (not too thinly as you want it to support the weight of the scallops).

To assemble, spoon a little tapenade onto each chorizo slice, put a seared scallop on top, and secure with a toothpick to serve.

butternut squash hot shots

Makes 40–50 shots

3 tablespoons olive oil

1 onion, chopped

5 garlic cloves, crushed

1 fresh red chile, seeded and chopped

1 teaspoon ras-el-hanout or mild curry powder

2¼ lbs. butternut squash, peeled, seeded, and chopped into chunks

4 cups vegetable stock

4 oz. half-dried tomatoes in olive oil, drained

1¼ cups fresh apple cider

1¼ cups sour cream

sea salt and freshly ground black pepper

shot glasses

Offer friends a warm welcome on cold, dark nights with these little soup shots, warm in color, taste, and temperature. Make sure your shot glasses are thick enough to contain hot liquids safely.

Heat the olive oil in a large, heavy-based saucepan and gently fry the onion, garlic, chile, and ras-el-hanout for a couple of minutes. Add the squash and fry for a further 5 minutes. Pour in the stock and cook for 10–12 minutes until the squash is tender. Remove from the heat and set aside to cool. Transfer the cooled squash to a food processor and add the tomatoes, apple cider, and half the cream. Blend until very smooth. Season to taste.

When you are ready to serve, reheat the soup and use the remaining sour cream to bring it to drinking consistency. Try one before serving; if the soup is too thick it will stay in the glass so add a little more cream or water to thin it further. You can also embellish the soup. Here are a few easy spiking suggestions:

• A crispy piece of pan-fried pancetta laid over the rim

• A couple of drops of white truffle oil on top

• A dash of Madeira or Marsala added just before serving

• A little cilantro oil and a few chopped leaves stirred in

• A few drops of sweet chili sauce added

• A thin wedge of Stilton balanced across the glass

sticks & skewers

spiced pork balls with sticky cider syrup

Makes 40–50

4 cups grapeseed oil

PORK BALLS

1 lb. ground pork

1 egg

2 teaspoons ground allspice

10 fresh sage leaves, chopped

4 scallions, chopped

1 teaspoon cayenne pepper

2 teaspoons sea salt

1 teaspoon caraway seeds

2 teaspoons tomato concentrate

2 tablespoons goose fat or
olive oil

CIDER SYRUP

2 cups hard apple cider

6 tablespoons balsamic vinegar

1 small fresh red or green chile

toothpicks

a shallow ovenproof dish

These subtly spiced pork balls are always a winner. The goose fat or olive oil keeps them succulent while cooking. If you have an electric deep-fat fryer, you'll find these even easier to make.

To make the pork balls, put all the ingredients in a large bowl and mix together thoroughly. Using clean hands, roll into 40–50 small balls and chill in the fridge for an hour.

For the cider syrup, put the cider and balsamic vinegar in a heavy-based saucepan, bring to a boil, then reduce the heat and simmer until reduced by about half to a syrupy consistency. Add the chile and leave to infuse. (Remember to remove the chile before serving.)

When you are ready to cook, preheat the oven to 400°F.

Pour the grapeseed oil into a deep, heavy-based saucepan and heat for deep-frying. To test the oil, drop in a crust of bread. If it sizzles immediately and turns golden brown it is ready; if it browns too much turn the heat down a little. Deep-fry the pork balls in 3 or 4 batches for a couple of minutes. Remove with a slotted spoon and drain on paper towels. Transfer to a shallow ovenproof dish and bake in the oven for a further 5–7 minutes until cooked all the way through. Serve on toothpicks with the sticky cider syrup in a small bowl for dipping.

broiled lamb skewers with garlic and saffron custard

Makes 30

1 lb. lamb loin fillet, cut into 30 cubes

2 tablespoons olive oil

1 tablespoon chopped fresh oregano

freshly ground black pepper

GARLIC AND SAFFRON CUSTARD

3 tablespoons butter

8–10 garlic cloves, coarsely grated

½ teaspoon saffron strands

2 cups heavy cream

grated peel and freshly squeezed juice of 1 small unwaxed lemon

sea salt

30 wooden skewers, about 6 inches long, soaked in water for 30 minutes before use

a baking sheet

The wonderful garlic and saffron sauce has the consistency of custard, but doesn't actually contain eggs. If the custard becomes too thick, dilute it with a little lemon juice or white wine.

Marinate the lamb in the olive oil, oregano, and black pepper for about 2 hours.

When you are ready to cook, preheat the broiler to medium. Thread the lamb cubes onto the prepared wooden skewers and put them on a baking sheet, loosely covering the sticks with foil to prevent them from scorching. Set aside.

To make the custard, gently heat the butter, garlic, and saffron together in a large, heavy-based frying pan. Add half the heavy cream and simmer until the cream bubbles and thickens. Add the lemon juice, and reduce the heat.

Broil the lamb skewers for 2–3 minutes on each side and keep warm until ready to serve.

Add the remaining cream, the grated lemon peel, and a little salt to the saffron cream mixture and stir over low heat until you have a custard-like sauce. Pour into a bowl and serve with the aromatic lamb skewers.

coconut and cardamom chicken

Makes 30–40

1 lb. skinless, boneless chicken breast meat, cubed

1¼ cups coconut cream

2 garlic cloves, crushed

1 small fresh red chile, seeded, and chopped

a 2-inch piece of fresh ginger, peeled and finely grated

1 star anise

seeds from 20 cardamom pods

2 teaspoons sea salt

TO SERVE

2 tablespoons onion seeds

a handful of cilantro, lightly chopped

6 long skewers, soaked in water for 30 minutes before use if wooden

a baking sheet

toothpicks

The coconut cream tenderizes the chicken, making it creamy and light, while cardamom adds an aromatic edge. It takes a little time to collect the cardamom seeds; use a rolling pin to crush the pods. These are luscious eaten hot or cold, so you could make them in advance, too.

Mix everything, except the salt, together in a bowl. Let marinate in the fridge for a few hours or overnight.

When you are ready to cook, preheat the oven to 400°F.

Add the salt to the chicken pieces and toss to mix, then thread them onto skewers. Arrange them in a single layer on a baking sheet. If you are using wooden skewers, cover them loosely with foil to prevent them from scorching. Cook in the oven for about 10 minutes until the chicken is cooked through.

Remove the chicken pieces from the skewers, scatter with the onion seeds and cilantro, and serve on toothpicks.

hot crumbed shrimp with tomato aioli

Makes 40

TOMATO AIOLI

3 egg yolks

2 garlic cloves

3 oz. half-dried tomatoes in oil, drained

freshly squeezed juice of 1 lemon

1 teaspoon tomato concentrate

2 cups olive oil

HOT CRUMBED SHRIMP

1 cup fresh bread crumbs

14 oz. jumbo shrimp, uncooked

grated peel and freshly squeezed juice of 2 unwaxed lemons

lemon wedges, to serve

sea salt

a baking sheet

toothpicks

Eat these lemon-drenched shrimp hot or cold with sweet tomato aioli. Alternatively, you can thread the shrimp onto skewers and cook them on an outdoor grill.

Preheat the broiler to high.

Put all the aioli ingredients, except the olive oil, in a food processor and blend. With the motor running, gradually trickle in the oil, very slowly at first, until you have a silky thick mayonnaise.

For the shrimp, lightly toast the bread crumbs under the hot broiler until crisp and golden. Watch carefully and do not let them burn. Combine the shrimp with the grated lemon peel and half the lemon juice in a bowl. Transfer the shrimp to a baking sheet and broil for 2–3 minutes, turning once, until they have turned from blue to pink.

Quickly pile the shrimp onto a serving plate. Sprinkle the remaining lemon juice over the shrimp, season with a little sea salt, and scatter the toasted bread crumbs over the top. Serve immediately with lemon wedges, toothpicks, and the tomato aioli for dipping.

piri piri mushrooms

Makes about 30

PIRI PIRI

2 large fresh red chiles

2 large garlic cloves

2 teaspoons sea salt crystals

2 teaspoons white wine vinegar

2 tablespoons olive oil

MUSHROOMS

2 tablespoons olive oil

1 garlic clove, crushed

14 oz. baby button mushrooms

a handful of fresh flat-leaf parsley, chopped

toothpicks

I found the inspiration for these in a small restaurant hidden among the eucalyptus trees up a mountain in the Algarve. Beware, they are hot!

Blend all the piri piri ingredients in a food processor until you have a smooth liquid.

For the mushrooms, gently heat the olive oil in a large saucepan, add the garlic, mushrooms, and half the parsley and cook over a medium heat for 3–4 minutes. Turn up the heat, add the piri piri mixture, and cook for a further 3–4 minutes, using a wooden spoon to stir the mushrooms and prevent them from sticking.

Scatter in the remaining parsley, stir, and serve straight away in a shallow dish with toothpicks on the side for spearing (just as you would if serving olives).

peppered duck, fig, and bay skewers

Makes 50

1 lb. lean duck breasts

2 garlic cloves crushed with
1 teaspoon sea salt

25 soft dried figs, halved

50 bay leaves

2 tablespoons olive oil

freshly ground black pepper

50 wooden skewers, soaked in water for 30 minutes before use

2 baking sheets

This one is favored by meat lovers and Francophiles. Use loin of lamb for a change or if you cannot find duck. For vegetarians, use big flat mushrooms. They look great on earthy yellow or terracotta dishes.

Preheat the oven to 400°F.

Cut the duck breasts into 50 strips of approximately the same size. Using clean hands, mix all the remaining ingredients together in a bowl, then add the duck strips and mix well.

Thread a duck strip and fig half on each skewer, with a bay leaf in between. Put the skewers on baking sheets, loosely covering the ends with foil to prevent them from scorching. Cook in the oven for 5–6 minutes, turning once, until the duck is tender and cooked through. Serve warm.

shrimp cocktail shots

These miniature shrimp cocktails are eye-catching and popular, and an up-to-date version of a Seventies classic. You will need small shot glasses and good-looking toothpicks.

Makes 30

¾ cup crème fraîche or sour cream

2 tablespoons tomato ketchup

2 teaspoons Manzanilla sherry

a small handful each of fresh tarragon leaves and fresh dill, chopped

1 teaspoon Spanish smoked paprika

a pinch of celery salt

2 scallions, chopped (optional)

14 oz. cooked and peeled jumbo shrimp (about 60), tails left on if liked

1 tablespoon snipped fresh chives or a pinch of Spanish smoked paprika, to garnish

shot glasses

toothpicks

To make the cocktail sauce, put the crème fraîche, ketchup, sherry, herbs, paprika, and celery salt in a small bowl. Mix with a fork or small whisk until well combined and smooth.

Spoon a little cocktail sauce into each shot glass and add a few chopped scallions, if using. Thread 2 shrimp onto each toothpick. Dip the shrimp into the remaining cocktail sauce, ensuring that the shrimp are coated, then carefully slide each stick into a shot glass, being careful not to smear sauce on the inside of the glass.

Garnish with either a sprinkling of chives or a pinch of smoked paprika, as preferred. Serve immediately.

twice-marinated
salt lime chicken

Makes 40

1 lb. skinless boneless
chicken thighs

3 tablespoons olive oil

a generous pinch of salt crystals

grated peel and freshly squeezed
juice of 2 unwaxed limes

non-metallic shallow dish

toothpicks

*Something magical happens when you put lime and salt together.
Whet guests' appetites with this zingy, salty chicken canapé.
Serve chilled with ice-cold beers and wines, or margaritas.*

Cut the chicken into 40 even chunks and put it in a
non-metallic dish with 1 tablespoon of the olive oil,
half the salt crystals, and the grated peel and juice of
1 lime. Let marinate in the fridge for 2 hours.

When you are ready to cook, remove the chicken from the
marinade. Heat the remaining olive oil in a frying pan and
sauté the chicken over medium heat for about 5 minutes
until cooked through, shaking the pan occasionally. Put
in a dish with the remaining salt and lime peel and juice.
Mix and chill for 1 hour before serving on toothpicks.

chicken salad kabobs

Makes 20

1 firm ripe mango, peeled
and pitted

1 small red onion, finely chopped

a few sprigs of cilantro, finely
chopped

1 firm ripe avocado, peeled
and pitted

freshly squeezed juice of ½ lime

8 oz. smoked chicken breast

10 dashes Angostura Bitters

½ teaspoon sea salt crystals

20 wooden satay sticks

*Bursting with fresh flavors and bright colors, these tangy skewers look
great in shallow white bowls. If you can find them, use satay sticks for
the kabobs. (See photograph on page 5.)*

Cut the mango into 20 cubes as neatly as possible and put in
a bowl with the red onion and cilantro. Mix to coat well.
Cut the avocado into 20 neat cubes and put in another
bowl with the lime juice. Finally, cut the smoked chicken
into 20 cubes and mix with the Angostura Bitters and salt.
Thread a cube each of avocado, mango, and chicken onto
the skewers and serve immediately.

spanish men

Makes 30

30 small Spanish olives, pitted
1 tablespoon extra virgin olive oil
1 tablespoon sherry vinegar
1 teaspoon Spanish smoked paprika
4 oz. Serrano ham, thinly sliced
1 tablespoon very finely chopped fresh flat-leaf parsley
5 oz. membrillo (quince paste), cut into 30 identically-sized cubes
5 oz. Manchego cheese, cut into 30 identically-sized cubes

toothpicks

For maximum visual impact, present these in neat rows. Spanish Men can be assembled well in advance and kept chilled. Don't push the toothpicks all the way through the cheese, or the men won't stand up!

Begin by marinating the olives in the olive oil, sherry vinegar, and smoked paprika for 1 hour or so.

Lay out the Serrano ham and rub the parsley over each slice. Cut into 30 equal-sized pieces (approximately 3 pieces from each slice). Roll up each small piece as tightly as possible into a cylinder and chill for 20 minutes.

Assemble the men by threading the components onto a toothpick in the following order: an olive, a cube of membrillo, a roll of ham, and a cube of Manchego.

manchego marinated with thyme and juniper

Makes about 30

8 oz. Manchego cheese
20 juniper berries
a sprig or 2 of fresh thyme
¾ cup extra virgin olive oil
a curl of orange peel

toothpicks

A good excuse to use your very best olive oil. Offer these simple yet indulgent shards of aromatic Manchego with toothpicks and napkins.

Cut the Manchego into approximately 30 shards and put in a shallow dish. Crush the juniper berries using a pestle and mortar or with a rolling pin and add them to the dish. Rub the thyme leaves onto the cheese, then tie the sprigs together and put them in the dish too. Pour the olive oil over, throw in the orange peel, and cover. Let the cheese marinate overnight in the fridge. To serve, bring to room temperature and remove the thyme sprigs and orange peel.

breads & crackers

smoked haddock and celeriac on pumpernickel with beet relish

Makes 30–40

BEETROOT RELISH

7 oz. cooked beet, finely diced

1 large shallot, finely chopped

1 tablespoon snipped fresh chives

2 tablespoons tomato concentrate

SMOKED HADDOCK AND CELERIAC

10 oz. smoked haddock fillet

7 oz. celeriac, peeled

3 tablespoons good-quality prepared mayonnaise or homemade

1 tablespoon horseradish sauce

1 lb. pumpernickel

fresh cilantro leaves, to garnish (optional)

a 2-inch cookie cutter (optional)

This is a colorful and unusual canapé. As an alternative to smoked haddock, you could also use smoked cod or mackerel. For vegetarians, you could use slices of hard-cooked egg.

To make the relish, put all the ingredients in a bowl and mix to combine. Cover and refrigerate until needed.

For the smoked haddock and celeriac, put the smoked haddock in a saucepan with just enough cold water to cover. Bring to a boil, reduce the heat, and let simmer for about 2 minutes until cooked, then drain and flake (removing any skin and little bones). Leave to cool.

Coarsely grate the celeriac or shred it in a food processor. Transfer to a bowl and stir in the mayonnaise, horseradish, and flaked haddock.

Cut the pumpernickel into 30–40 rounds using a 2-inch cookie cutter (or squares, if preferred). Spoon a little haddock and celeriac mixture onto each one. Using a clean spoon, pile a little beet relish on top and garnish with a cilantro leaf, if using, to finish. Serve immediately.

anchovy wafers

Ready-made salty snacks pall beside these crumbly melt-on-the-tongue wafers. They deserve to be paired with well-chilled dry Champagne. If you serve these, balance them with something sour or sweet.

1 cup all-purpose flour

1 stick chilled butter, cubed

1¼ cups grated sharp cheddar cheese

2 tablespoons chopped fresh sweet marjoram or 2 teaspoons dried oregano

4 oz. anchovies in olive oil, drained and halved lengthwise

freshly ground black pepper

parchment paper

baking sheets

Sift the flour onto a clean counter, make a well in the center and add the butter, cheese, herbs, and black pepper. With clean, cool fingers, rub together to form a soft, tacky dough. Scoop the dough up, with the aid of a spatula if necessary, and put it on a large piece of parchment paper. Mold the mixture into a flattish rectangle, wrap up in the paper, and chill for 1 hour in the fridge.

Preheat the oven to 400°F. Using a sharp knife, cut the dough (just as you would slice a loaf of bread) into thin wafers and arrange them on baking sheets, positioning them not too close together. Lay an anchovy half lengthwise on each wafer and bake for 8 minutes until golden. Let cool on a wire rack.

parmesan and sweet paprika crackers

Makes 40 biscuits

1¼ cups finely grated Parmesan cheese

1 stick chilled butter, cubed

1 cup all-purpose flour, plus extra for dusting

2 teaspoons sweet paprika

2 teaspoons Dijon mustard

sea salt

freshly ground black pepper

a 2-inch cookie cutter

2 baking sheets

waxed paper

These delicate mouthfuls bring the classic cheese cracker right up to date. They are smoky, dry, and tempting and go perfectly with a glass of Prosecco. Be careful not to overcook them, or they will taste bitter.

Put all the ingredients in a food processor and process briefly until the mixture forms a dough ball. Wrap the dough in waxed paper and chill in the fridge for 1 hour.

Preheat the oven to 400°F. Dust a clean counter and a rolling pin with flour and roll out the dough to approximately ¼ inch thick. Using a 2-inch cookie cutter, stamp out 40 crackers and put them on baking sheets. Bake for 8 minutes, checking after 6 minutes to make sure the crackers are not darkening in color.

Remove from the oven, leave for a couple of minutes, then very carefully lift the crackers onto a wire rack to cool and crisp up before serving.

flash-seared tuna on rye with horseradish and tarragon cream

Makes 20

2 tablespoons olive oil

1 teaspoon soft brown sugar

a 16-oz piece of fresh tuna loin, thin end

¾ cup crème fraîche or sour cream

2 tablespoons horseradish sauce

1 carrot, grated

2 tablespoons chopped fresh tarragon, plus 20 whole leaves to serve

10 oz. rye bread, cut into 20 fingers

sea salt and freshly ground black pepper

a stovetop grill pan

The richness of fresh tuna is complemented here by the sharpness of the horseradish and the aniseed pungency of tarragon. With the rye bread base, this is a substantial canapé.

In a wide, shallow bowl, mix the olive oil, sugar, and a little salt and black pepper together, then add the tuna loin and turn carefully until coated.

Heat a stovetop grill pan over high heat until very hot. Add the tuna and, using tongs to turn it over, sear on all sides for about 1 minute. Remove from the heat and let it cool slightly before cutting into 20 thin even slices.

Mix the crème fraîche, horseradish, carrot, and chopped tarragon together in a separate bowl. Season with salt and black pepper and spread on the rye bread fingers. Top each with a slice of seared tuna and a tarragon leaf and serve immediately.

Note: if you prefer to eat tuna medium to well done, simply return the slices to the pan and sear for a further 30 seconds to 1 minute, until cooked as desired.

cheese scones with cheddar and pickled pears

Makes 30

PICKLED PEARS

1½ lbs. firm pears

1½ cups soft brown sugar

2 cups cider vinegar

½ onion studded with 4 cloves

2 bay leaves, bruised

1 cinnamon stick

CHEESE SCONES

3¾ cups self-rising flour, plus extra for dusting

1 stick plus 2 tablespoons butter

1 cup grated sharp cheddar cheese

2 teaspoons salt

2 teaspoons baking soda

1 teaspoon Dijon mustard

1 teaspoon cayenne pepper

¾ cup milk

7 oz. sharp cheddar cheese, shaved into rough thin slices

a 1½-inch cookie cutter

baking sheets

Gruyère could be substituted for the cheddar in this recipe. These little scones are particularly good served warm and filled at the last minute. If you have any leftover pickled pears you could serve them with cold meats or a cheese platter.

For the pickled pears, peel, quarter and core the pears. Put all the other ingredients in a large saucepan and gently bring to a boil. When the sugar has dissolved, add the pears and simmer for about 5–8 minutes until just tender. Remove the pears from the liquid with a slotted spoon and transfer them to a shallow dish. Set aside to cool. Continue boiling the liquid until it reduces by half and becomes a syrup. Discard the onion, bay leaves, and cinnamon and gently pour the syrup over the pears to coat.

Preheat the oven to 400°F. To make the scones, rub the flour and butter together in a bowl until it resembles fine bread crumbs then add ½ cup of the grated cheese. Add the salt, baking soda, Dijon mustard, and cayenne pepper and mix to combine. Next add enough milk to bring the dry ingredients together and form a pliable dough. Be prudent—you may not need it all. Flour a clean counter, turn the dough out, and knead it lightly. Pat it out to a thickness of ½ inch Stamp out rounds approximately 1½ inches wide, sprinkle the remaining grated cheese over the scones, transfer to baking sheets, and bake for 10 minutes until lightly browned. Let cool a little on a wire rack. Slice the pickled pears into small pieces. Cut the scones ¾ of the way through, put a slice of cheese and a piece of pickled pear inside and serve.

arugula sandwiches

Makes 24

10 oz. cream cheese

2 garlic cloves, crushed

1 tablespoon freshly squeezed lemon juice

4 oz. arugula

12 medium slices fresh whole-grain bread

⅓ cup toasted sunflower seeds

sea salt crystals

These lively little sandwiches are packed with peppery nutrition and are quick to put together using a food processor. Serve them with sweet, ripe cherry tomatoes for a color and flavor contrast.

Put the cream cheese, garlic, lemon juice, and half the arugula in a food processor and whizz together for about 10 seconds. Spread the mixture evenly over all the bread slices and sprinkle with a pinch of salt.

Scatter the sunflower seeds and remaining arugula onto half the slices, then top with the rest of the bread.

Cut the crusts off if desired and cut each sandwich into triangles or squares, as preferred. Cover tightly with plastic wrap until ready to serve to prevent the bread from drying out and curling.

oak-smoked salmon with ginger butter on oat biscuits

Makes 30

OAT BISCUITS

¾ cup all-purpose flour

¾ cup rolled oats

1 teaspoon salt

6½ tablespoons chilled butter, grated

GINGER BUTTER AND OAK-SMOKED SALMON TOPPING

6½ tablespoons butter, softened

a 1½-inch piece of fresh ginger, peeled and finely chopped

10-12 fresh chives

7 oz. oak-smoked salmon

cracked black pepper (optional)

parchment paper

a 1½-inch cookie cutter

baking sheets

You can bake the oat biscuits in advance and assemble them at the last minute. Handle the biscuits with care as they are crumbly. To cut the richness, serve with bowls of vinegary onions and baby gherkins.

To make the oat biscuits, put all the ingredients in a large bowl and mix together. Add a little water to bring the mixture together, but don't allow the dough to become soggy. Chill in the fridge for 20 minutes.

Preheat the oven to 375°F.

Roll the pastry out thinly between 2 pieces of parchment paper or in a large freezer bag. Cut out 30 rounds using a 1½-inch cookie cutter, put on baking sheets, and bake for about 10 minutes. The biscuits will not color much. Lift them off carefully and let cool on a wire rack.

To make the ginger butter, put the butter, ginger, and chives in a food processor and blend until smooth. Using a spatula, spoon the butter mixture into a bowl.

To assemble, tear off a piece of smoked salmon, smear with a little ginger butter, and place on top of each oat biscuit. Sprinkle over a little cracked black pepper to serve, if liked.

sweet treats

rose marzipan dates

Makes 50

25 plump fresh dates
1⅓ cups ground almonds
⅔ cup confectioners' sugar, sifted
freshly squeezed lemon juice
2 tablespoons rosewater

TO DECORATE
superfine sugar
freshly toasted slivered almonds,
chopped
fresh rose petals, crystallized
roses or dried rosebuds

*Luxuriate in the delicate, subtle character of these romantic flavors.
As well as toasted almonds, try decorating the dates with fresh edible
roses, crystallized roses or dried rosebuds, or rolling them in sugar.*

Slit the dates open lengthwise and remove the pits. Put the
ground almonds and confectioners' sugar in a large bowl.
Make a well in the center and add a little lemon juice
and the rosewater. Gradually combine the dry and wet
ingredients, using a cold fork to work the mixture into a
firm paste. It may appear initially that there is not enough
moisture, but eventually the almonds will release their
natural oils.

Divide the marzipan equally between the dates and
decorate as desired.

fudgy nuts

Serves about 30

1 stick butter
2½ cups superfine sugar
1 cup condensed milk
2 teaspoons coffee essence or
2 teaspoons freshly-made, strong
espresso coffee
1 lb. mixed nuts, such as unsalted
pistachios, pecans, brazils, and
almonds

a baking sheet, lightly greased

*Be prepared to stir and beat the mixture for a while until you create
a heavenly fudge, then just try and stop yourself from eating all of these
deliciously sweet nuts before your guests arrive!*

Put the butter and sugar in a large, heavy-based saucepan
with 1¼ cups water and set the pan over low heat. Bring
to a boil, stirring all the time. Boil for 2 minutes then add
the condensed milk and simmer for 20–30 minutes, again
stirring all the time. Remove from the heat, add the coffee
essence, and beat for 10 minutes until the fudge thickens
and loses its gloss. Stir in the nuts, pile the mixture onto a
lightly greased baking sheet, and let cool. Break into lumps
and serve in bowls.

orange and chocolate marble cake

Makes about 24 slices

2 sticks plus 2 tablespoons butter

¾ cup superfine sugar

3 large eggs

¾ cup all-purpose flour

1 teaspoon baking powder

½ cup ground almonds

grated peel of 1 small unwaxed orange

1 teaspoon orange flower water

1 oz. bittersweet chocolate, grated

1 tablespoon unsweetened cocoa powder

confectioners' sugar, for dredging

whipped cream, to serve

4 mini loaf pans or a small ring mold, buttered and coated with ground almonds

These pretty little slices of cake make a perfect bite-size indulgence to follow a feast of savory canapés. Serve with a bowl brimming with whipped cream and a spoon so that your guests can help themselves.

Preheat the oven to 350°F.

In a large bowl, cream the butter and caster sugar together. Add the eggs 1 at a time, while continuing to beat. Sift the flour with the baking powder and fold in, then fold in the ground almonds.

Divide the mixture into two parts, one slightly larger than the other. Mix the grated orange peel and orange flower water into the larger half. Mix the grated chocolate and cocoa powder into the smaller half. Spoon half the orange mixture into the base of the prepared mini loaf pans, followed by the chocolate mixture and finishing with the remaining orange mixture. Bake for 40–45 minutes.

Remove from the oven and leave to cool for 5 minutes, then dredge the tops with confectioners' sugar. Turn out onto a wire rack and let cool completely before cutting into slices (you should get at least 6 from each mini loaf). Serve with a bowl of whipped cream.

mini meringues brushed with bitter chocolate

Makes 40–50

3 egg whites

¼ teaspoon cream of tartar

¾ cup plus 2 tablespoons superfine or granulated sugar

7 oz. bittersweet chocolate (60–70% cocoa solids), broken into small pieces

gold edible paint or edible glitter (optional)

a piping bag with fluted tip

baking sheets lined with baking parchment

a soft pastry brush

Elegant clouds of meringue brushed with rich, bittersweet chocolate. When the chocolate has set, gently smudge edible gold or glitter over the chocolate to catch the light and sparkle.

Preheat the oven to 250°F.

Put the egg whites in a clean, grease-free bowl and beat with an electric whisk until stiff. Add the cream of tartar and beat again. Very slowly add the sugar, beating constantly, until all the sugar is incorporated and you have a thick, glossy and silky mixture.

Fill a piping bag fitted with a fluted tip with the mixture and pipe little "tongues", each about 3 inches long, onto a baking sheet lined with baking parchment. Bake for 30 minutes, then turn the oven temperature down to 225°F and continue baking for a further 2 hours until the meringues are dry.

When you are ready to decorate the meringues, put them on a wire rack. Set a heat-proof bowl over a pan filled with boiling water, making sure the bowl does not touch the water. Put the chocolate in the bowl and leave it to melt slowly. When it has melted, brush a lick of chocolate down the length of each meringue using a soft pastry brush. Let cool and set, then smudge on a little gold edible paint, if liked. Serve on a glass dish for impact.

snowy pine nut cookies

Makes about 20

1 stick plus 5 tablespoons butter, softened

½ cup superfine or granulated sugar

1½ cups all-purpose flour

½ teaspoon sea salt

1¼ pine nuts, roughly chopped

1 teaspoon pure almond extract (optional)

confectioners' sugar, for dredging

baking sheets

Rich, buttery and addictive to the nut nut! Dredge with confectioners' sugar while warm and again when cold before serving with dessert wines, sticky liqueurs, or spicy mulled wine.

Preheat the oven to 350°F.

Put the butter and superfine sugar in a large bowl and beat together until soft. Add the flour, salt, pine nuts, and almond extract, if using, and mix well to combine.

Using your hands, form the mixture into small balls about 1½ inches in diameter and place them slightly apart on baking sheets as they will spread during baking. Bake for 12–15 minutes (they won't color much).

Let cool a little before transferring to a wire rack and dredging with confectioners' sugar. Dredge again when the cookies are cold and you are about to serve them.

apple and calvados pies

Makes 24

PASTRY

2 cups all-purpose flour, plus extra for dusting

1 stick chilled butter, cubed

½ cup confectioners' sugar

1 egg

seeds from ½ vanilla bean

1 tablespoon Calvados (French apple brandy)

fresh walnut halves, to decorate (optional)

milk, to glaze

confectioners' sugar, for dredging

FILLING

3½ oz. Calvados

1½ lbs. eating apples, peeled, cored, and finely chopped or roughly grated

¾ cup raw cane sugar

5 tablespoons butter

seeds from ½ vanilla bean

2½ and 2-inch cookie cutters

2 x 12-hole mini muffin pans

These are delicious served with gooey cheeses, as an alternative to mincemeat pies, or with a big bowl of whipped cream. Introduce a little variation by replacing some of the lids with a fresh walnut half.

First make the pastry. Put the flour, butter, and confectioners' sugar in a food processor and process until the mixture resembles fine bread crumbs. Mix the egg with the vanilla seeds and Calvados and add to the mixture. Process quickly until it forms a lump of dough, then wrap in plastic wrap and chill in the fridge for 30 minutes.

Preheat the oven to 400°F.

To prepare the filling, put the apples in a bowl and splash the Calvados over the top. Leave to stand for 10 minutes. Put the apples in a heavy-based saucepan with the muscovado sugar, butter, and vanilla seeds and set over medium heat. Cook until the apples are tender and the liquid has evaporated, stirring occasionally.

Lightly flour a clean counter and roll out the chilled pastry carefully. Stamp out 24 rounds using a 2½ inch cookie cutter and use them to line the mini muffin pans. Using a teaspoon, fill the pies with the apple filling; pack them quite full, but do not heap. Stamp out the remaining pastry using a 2 inch cookie cutter and press lightly onto the pies. If you run out of pastry for the lids, top some of the pies with a walnut half. Brush sparingly with milk and bake for 20–25 minutes. Cool on a wire rack and dredge with confectioners' sugar to serve.

peppered pineapple, coconut, and rum shots

Serves 10–15 depending on
the size of the glasses

16 oz. very ripe prepared fresh
pineapple flesh

¾ cup coconut cream

3½ oz. white rum

2 tablespoons muscovado sugar

¼ teaspoon sea salt

TO SERVE

freshly grated nutmeg

freshly ground black pepper

cayenne pepper

shot or aperitif glasses

Reviving! Chill the ingredients before you make these, then they are ready to serve straight away. Alternatively, you can freeze the mixture, crush it, and serve it as a granita. Be warned, the cayenne is very pungent so only use it if you know that your guests like things hot!

Put the pineapple, coconut cream, rum, sugar, and salt in a blender or food processor and whizz until smooth and creamy. Transfer the mixture to a pitcher and carefully pour it into small shot glasses to serve.

To finish, you can either grate over a little nutmeg, add a few grinds of black pepper or add a sprinkling of cayenne, as preferred.

index